DINOSAUR LADY

The Daring Discoveries of Mary Anning, the First Paleontologist

words by Linda Skeers

pictures by Marta Álvarez Miguéns

Mary Anning dodged high tides and crashing waves to scour the beach near her hometown of Lyme Regis, England. She filled her basket with "curiosities" to sell to tourists, like seashells and fossils with fanciful local names like "snake-stones" (ammonites), "devil toenails" (belemnites), and "angel wings" (*Petricola pholadiformis*).

She scrambled over crumbling cliffs and rocky peaks while avoiding life-threatening landslides.

Despite the constant danger, Mary wasn't afraid. She was determined to uncover the area's long-buried secrets—no matter the risk.

Mary learned to read and write at Sunday school, but she wanted to learn more. She had so many questions about the bones and fossils she found, and she needed answers!

She borrowed books and copied scientific papers. She sketched intricate drawings of her discoveries, and she made notes.

Lots and lots of notes.

One morning, when Mary and her brother were exploring the cliffs, they saw something surprising. Nestled in the rock was a large eye socket looking right back at them!

Carefully, they chiseled away dirt and stone to expose a four-foot-long head with a pointed snout.

Massive jaw.

Hundreds of teeth.

It was frightening!

But Mary wasn't scared. She was fascinated!

They coaxed workers from the village to help dig it out
and carry it home.

While the men returned to their work, Mary set out to find the creature's body. The cliffs were constantly shifting and sliding. It had to be buried nearby.

But where?

Day after day, Mary scrambled over the cliffs.

Week after week she searched.

Month after month.

After almost a year, Mother Nature lent Mary a helping hand. The powerful wind and pounding rain from a devastating storm caused several landslides.

In one night, the cliff's ancient layers were exposed.
Layers that would have taken Mary years to uncover
with her hammer and chisel.

Something caught Mary's eye.

Bones.

Boldly, Mary chipped away…
and uncovered ribs.

Vertebrae.

Flippers!

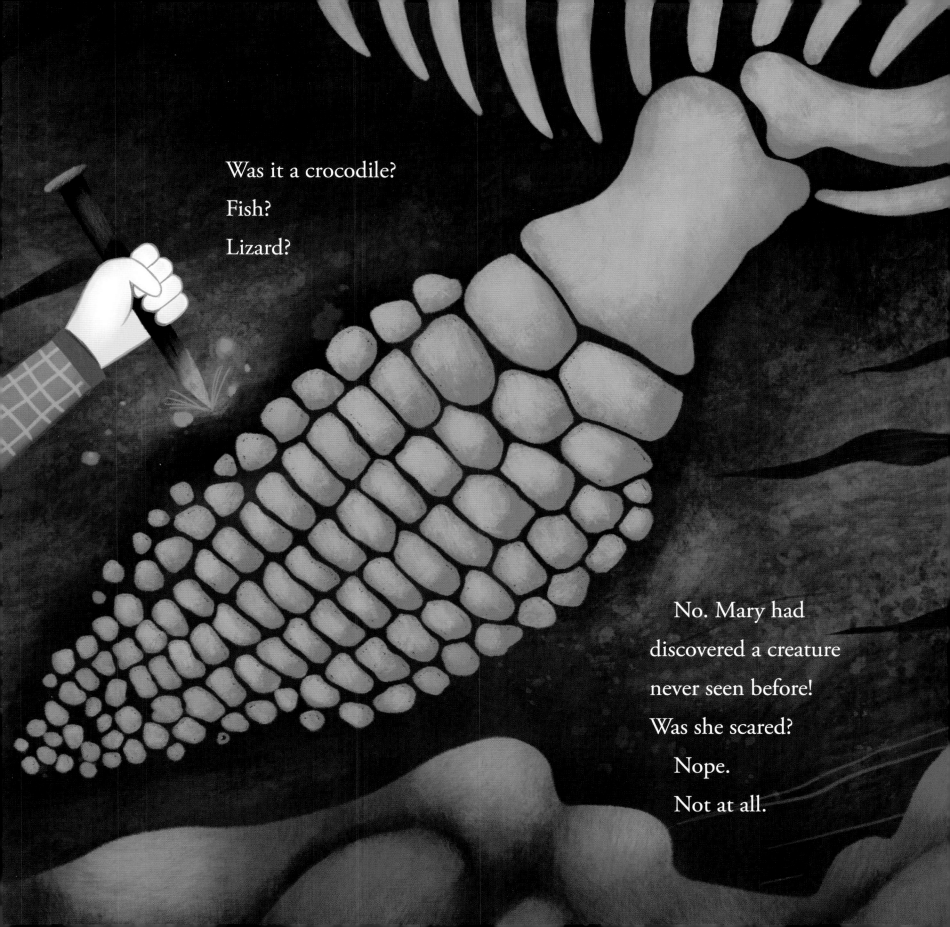

Was it a crocodile?

Fish?

Lizard?

No. Mary had
discovered a creature
never seen before!
Was she scared?
Nope.
Not at all.

But many villagers were. Soon they were talking about "Mary's Monster." Word traveled to a rich collector who offered to buy the skeleton. Mary hated to see it go, but the money would help the Anning family survive for months.

The collector donated it to a London museum and scientists and geologists flocked to the exhibit.

They studied it.

Calculated.

Debated.

They named it *Ichthyosaurus*, which meant "fish lizard." The word "dinosaur" hadn't even been invented yet.

They made an announcement that shocked the world.

Mary's find wasn't just old, it was *millions* of years old!

Their declaration shattered the commonly held belief that the Earth was only six thousand years old.

Also, no one had realized that a species could become extinct until they studied the remains of a creature that no longer walked the Earth.

While others discussed her discovery,
Mary kept exploring.
And learning.

Over the years, Mary also found many odd, dark, lumpy
pebbles inside skeletons.

She examined them.

Reread her notes.

Studied her drawings.

Mary figured out what they were!

Except it was something a lady shouldn't talk about…

But Mary was more of a scientist than a proper lady,
so she proclaimed these stones, known as bezoars, were
actually fossilized POOP!

Geologists sneered.

Scientists scoffed.

Then they took a closer look and realized she was right! Mary's discovery helped scholars learn more about what ancient creatures ate.

Mary also found many long, thin, cone-shaped fossils.

They were unremarkable.

Ordinary.
At least, on the outside.
Curious, she cut one open.

Tucked inside was a small pocket filled with a thick, dark substance.

Mary was even more curious now!

Adding a few drops of water turned the substance into...

INK.

Mary's discovery proved that ancient aquatic creatures squirted ink to hide themselves from hungry predators.

When Mary was twenty-four, she made another amazing discovery!

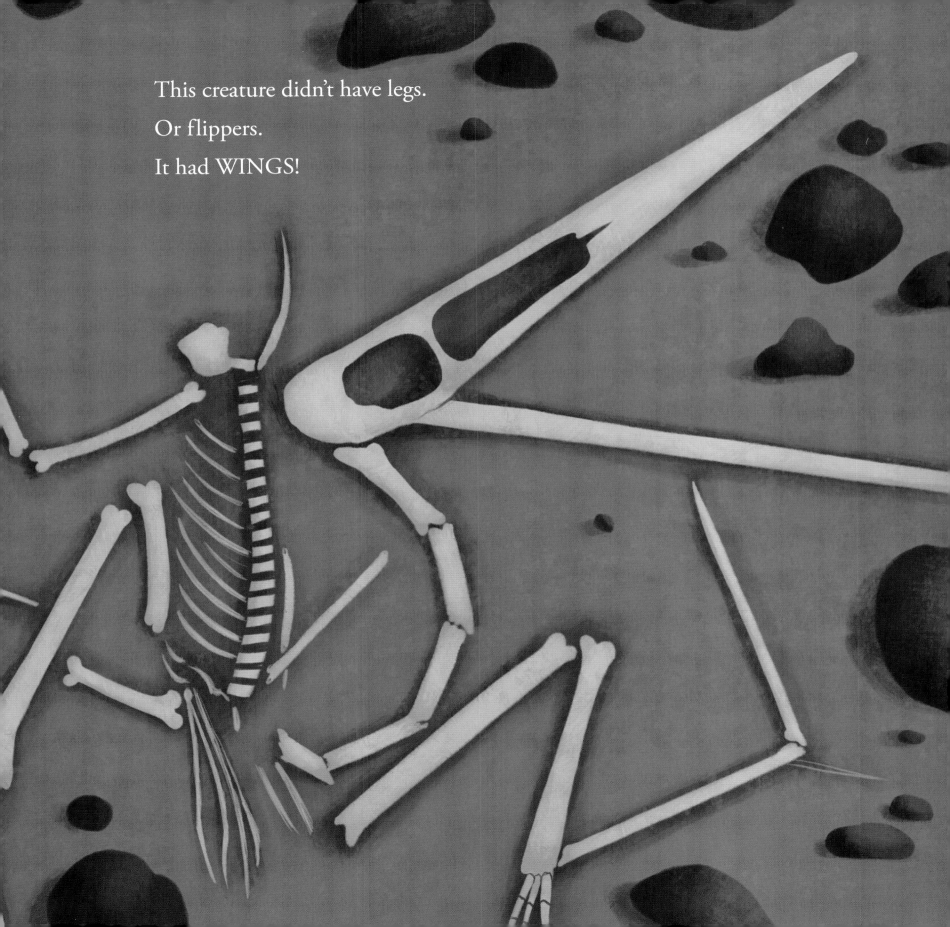

This creature didn't have legs.
Or flippers.
It had WINGS!

Mary had unearthed a prehistoric flying reptile called a pterosaur.

Around the world, scientists were talking about Mary's incredible discoveries.

But they weren't talking about Mary.

Not at first.

Even though Mary could identify a species from one single bone and rebuild entire skeletons like a jigsaw puzzle, she couldn't join the Geological Society of London. Women were not allowed.

She couldn't attend lectures or teach university classes. Or even take classes!

LECTURE HALL

But Mary knew her discoveries were important and would change the way people viewed the Earth's past.

And so did many geologists, scientists, and scholars. Because where did they go when they had questions?

Straight to Mary's cottage!

Eager to learn more, they followed her over the cliffs, even if it terrified them (and it did!).

Just like long-buried fossils, Mary's achievements have slowly been uncovered and shared with the world. Her daring discoveries helped form paleontology—the branch of geology that uses fossils to study prehistoric life.

And she did all that with a homemade hammer, a chisel, and a never-ending quest to fearlessly keep exploring—and learning.

BONE BITS
— AND —
FOSSIL FACTS

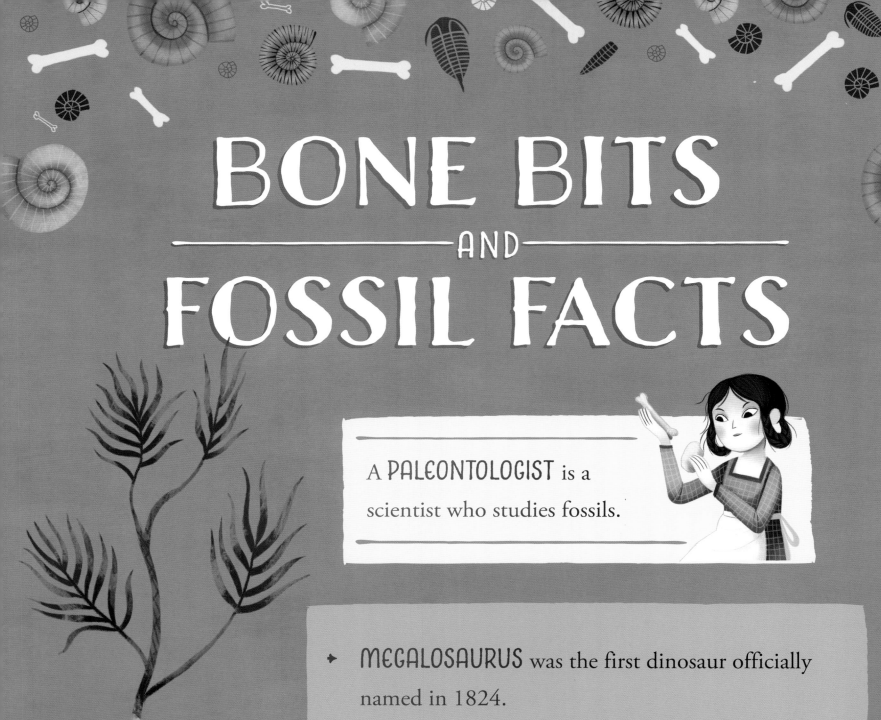

A **PALEONTOLOGIST** is a scientist who studies fossils.

+ **MEGALOSAURUS** was the first dinosaur officially named in 1824.

+ In 1842, paleontologist Richard Owen coined the term **DINOSAUR**, from the Greek **DEINOS** meaning "terrible" and **SAURUS** meaning "lizard."

Over seven hundred different kinds of dinosaurs have been discovered and named.

A **FOSSIL**— Latin for "having been dug up"— is the remains of an animal or plant that has turned to rock over many years.

An **AMMONITE** is a prehistoric sea creature with a spiral shell often found on beaches.

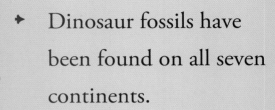

A **BELEMNITE** is a prehistoric sea creature like a squid, which squirts ink to defend itself from predators.

+ Dinosaur fossils have been found on all seven continents.

+ Some dinosaur eggs were as small as your thumbnail, others the size of basketballs.

PETRICOLA PHOLADIFORMIS is a type of clam also known as the "false angel wing" because its ribbed white shells resemble angel wings.

COPROLITES is the fancy name for fossilized poop. Also known as bezoars, they were at one time thought to have all sorts of medicinal properties!

MARY ANNING TIMELINE

1810
Mary's father, Richard Anning, dies.

1811
Mary and her brother discover an *Ichthyosaurus*.

MAY 21, 1799
Mary Anning is born in Lyme Regis, England.

AUGUST 19, 1800
Baby Mary is struck by lightning and survives.

1824
Mary announces that bezoar stones are actually fossilized poop!

1823
Mary discovers the first complete *Plesiosaurus*.

1826

Mary discovers a belemnite fossil containing dried ink.

Mary opens "Anning's Fossil Depot."

1828

Mary discovers a pterosaur—a prehistoric flying reptile that later became known as *Pterodactylus macronyx*.

MARCH 9, 1847

Mary dies of breast cancer at age forty-seven.

1829

Mary goes to London—her first and only trip out of Lyme Regis.

Mary discovers *Squaloraja polyspondyla*—a fish believed to be an evolutionary link between sharks and rays.

1844

King Frederick Augustus II of Saxony visits Mary in her shop.

2010

The Royal Society of London names Mary Anning one of the ten most influential British women of science.

AUTHOR'S NOTE

Even as a young girl, Mary had the uncanny ability to spot a small fossil, seashell, or bone fragment that others overlooked. She used this skill when she accompanied her father on his scavenging trips. Her father was a carpenter and cabinetmaker who supplemented his meager earnings by finding seashells and fossils to sell to tourists vacationing in the area, taking in the sea air. Mary was looking for trinkets to sell but she was also looking for answers to questions that baffled her. What created these strange-looking fossils? Where did they come from? What were they? She spent her entire life exploring, studying, and learning. Without any formal education, and relying on her own observations, intricate drawings, and meticulous notes, she became an expert on prehistoric creatures, earning the nickname "Princess of Paleontology."

Mary also lived in one of the best fossil-hunting places on Earth! Lyme Regis is part of the Jurassic Coast and was underwater two hundred million years ago. Storms and winter weather erode and crumble the cliffs, exposing fossils and bones. Mary didn't use special equipment—just a hammer her father had made, a chisel, and a hat that she had shellacked so many times it was hard as a helmet.

Mary's father died when she was eleven, thrusting Mary, her fourteen-year-old brother, Joseph, and their mother even deeper into poverty. Mary's "curiosities" now helped pay the rent and buy food.

During her lifetime, Mary made five major discoveries of previously unknown species and several smaller but still significant finds that helped change the way people looked at the world, and helped them better understand the past.

When Mary was only twenty-four, she discovered the first complete *Plesiosaurus*, an aquatic creature with flippers that was such an astonishing find, paleontologist Georges Cuvire declared it a fraud! But after he examined it, he proclaimed, "It is the most amazing creature ever discovered."

By the time Mary was twenty-seven, she had managed to save up enough money to buy a cottage with a glass storefront window and turned the front room into a shop called "Anning's Fossil Depot." She proudly displayed her discoveries in the window. It was so unusual for a woman to become a shopkeeper and own her own business that it made headlines in the local newspaper.

This tongue twister written in 1908 is said to be about Mary Anning:

She sells seashells on the seashore,
the shells she sells are seashells, I'm sure.
For if she sells seashells on the seashore,
then I'm sure she sells seashore shells.

Her portrait now hangs in the Natural History Museum in London.

The British Journal for the History of Science considers Mary Anning "the greatest fossilist the world ever knew."

BIBLIOGRAPHY

American Association for the Advancement of Science. "May 21: Today in Science." ScienceNetLinks. http://sciencenetlinks.com/daily-content/5/21/.

American Museum of Natural History. "Happy Birthday, Mary Anning! 'Princess of Paleontology'." AMNH Blog, May 21, 2014. https://www.amnh.org/explore /news-blogs/on-exhibit-posts/happy-birthday-mary-anning.

BBC. "Mary Anning – Fossil Hunter." BBC Bitesize. Updated April 14, 2018. https://www.bbc.co.uk/bitesize/topics/zd8fv9q/articles/zf6vb82.

Bechko, Corinna and Shawn McManus. "She Sold Science by the Seashore," in *Femme Magnifique: 50 Magnificent Women Who Changed the World*, edited by Shelly Bond, 13–16. New York: Black Crown, 2018.

Emling, Shelley. *The Fossil Hunter: Dinosaurs, Evolution, and the Woman Whose Discoveries Changed the World*. New York: St. Martin's Press, 2011.

Famousscientists.org. "Mary Anning." Famous Scientists. Updated October 26, 2016. http://www.famousscientists.org/mary-anning/.

Favilli, Elena and Francesca Cavallo. *Good Night Stories for Rebel Girls: 100 Tales of Extraordinary Women*. New York: Simon & Schuster, 2016.

Fradin, Dennis. *Mary Anning: The Fossil Hunter*. New York: Silver Burdett Press, 1997.

Huntington, Tom. "The Princess of Paleontology." *British Heritage Travel*, July 13, 2016. https://britishheritage.com/the-princess-of-paleontology.

Pierce, Patricia. *Jurassic Mary: Mary Anning and the Primeval Monsters*. Stroud, UK: The History Press, 2014.

TheSchoolRun. "Mary Anning." Updated January 21, 2015. https://www.theschoolrun.com/homework-help/mary-anning.

Snedden, Robert. *Mary Anning: Fossil Hunter*. New York: Gareth Stevens, 2016.

Tickell, Crispin. *Mary Anning of Lyme Regis*. Lyme Regis, UK: Lyme Regis Philpot Museum, 1996.

For my fearless sister, Cindy. Your courage and optimism inspires me every day.

—LS

Published by Sourcebooks eXplore, an imprint of Sourcebooks Kids
P.O. Box 4410, Naperville, Illinois 60567–4410
(630) 961-3900
sourcebookskids.com

Library of Congress Cataloging-in-Publication Data is on file with the publisher.

Source of Production: 1010 Printing Asia Limited, North Point, Hong Kong, China
Date of Production: November 2020
Run Number: 5020461

Printed and bound in China.
OGP 10 9 8 7 6 5 4 3 2